AF427963

Autumn Shedding

Autumn Shedding

A Collection of Poetry by

Christian Ryan Pike

Published by Wheelsong Books

Plymouth, United Kingdom

First Published by
Wheelsong Books
4 Willow Close
Plymouth PL3 6EY
United Kingdom

Cover art © Reece Grooms, 2022
Book layout and design © Christian Ryan Pike, 2022

First Published in 2022

Print ISBN: 979-8-83505-712-2

Consider and hear me,

O Lord my God:

lighten mine eyes,

lest I sleep the sleep of death;

The Prophet David

Psalm 13:3

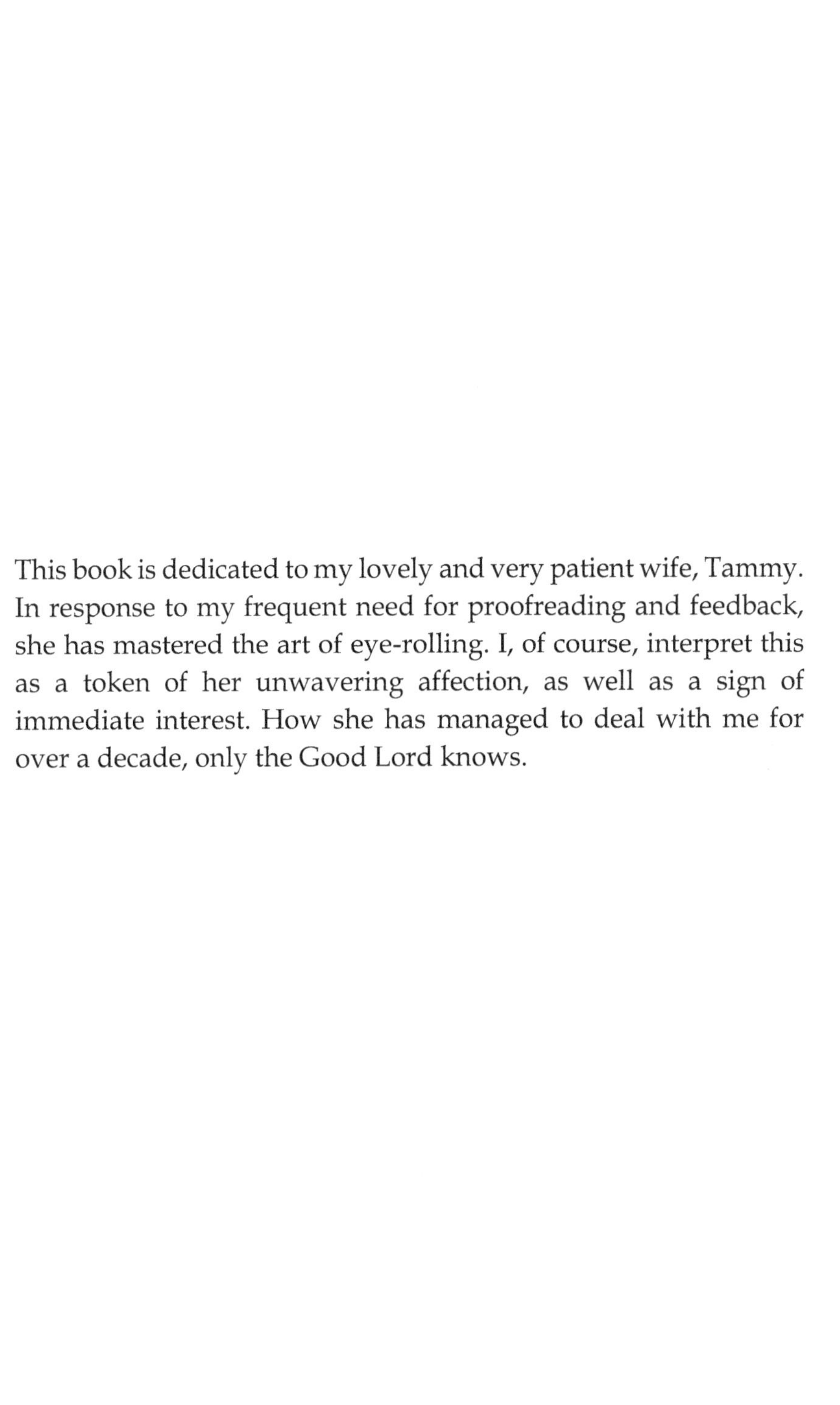

This book is dedicated to my lovely and very patient wife, Tammy. In response to my frequent need for proofreading and feedback, she has mastered the art of eye-rolling. I, of course, interpret this as a token of her unwavering affection, as well as a sign of immediate interest. How she has managed to deal with me for over a decade, only the Good Lord knows.

PART 1: Of Leaves & Leisure

PART 3: The Clause of Charity

PART 4: Intellectual Evening

PART 5: Some Poetic Somethings

PART 1: *Of Leaves & Leisure*

Autumn Shedding

Greenish-yellow hills roll over
Lucky like a four-leaf clover
Just to see a pink sun setting
And the leaves of autumn shedding

And I'm betting that in time
A festive moon will start to shine
Illuminating with a glow
A field of corn in planted row

A time to grow a pumpkin patch
Or wade out for a trout to catch
And ever so inviting still
Are shivers by a windy chill

Alas, to feel that winter looms
To sweep away with frigid brooms
The color palette, auburn dale
Replacing with a whiter vale

So Much More

The crescent moon is barely hanging
Right above the tree
Hollowed out and hallowed, glowing
Dimly lit with little showing
Full of knowledge, never knowing
So much by degree
There so much more to be
When angled light is casting phases
Strangling what so amazes
Like the razor's edge to graze
There's so much more to see

Winter Wear

Something aimless
Somewhat seasonal, but blameless
Also pairing rather nicely
With the flavorless and icy

Something dreary
Sort of lingering and leery
When you want to disappear
'Til the weather's in the clear

Something colder
Like the look over your shoulder
Where the scenery behind
Is the same of what you'll find

Something moving
As a gradient, improving
It'll come before you know
Like a flower through the snow

Honeysuckles

On rare occasions, when the mood's just right
Riding the breeze on a summer night
Hiding discreetly, yet in plain sight
An aroma that's suited for clear moonlight

It sets the tone that we hold so dear
A sweet remembrance that's made each year
Of stirring thoughts which reappear
Purifying the atmosphere

As honeysuckle so wildly grows
And sends a message to tempt your nose
Inspiring this, and other prose
Exalting fields where you arose

Taking us back to times when we
Would soak up life deliciously
Forever young, forever free
Embracing what we're made to be

And isn't it a crying shame
That somewhere, somehow, things have changed
We used to laugh, we now complain
We used to love, we now refrain

We used to dance, we used to sing
We used to hug, to hold and cling
We used to bid farewell to Spring
When hearts were broken just like strings

When tenderness held us as one
With memories made in the sun
Of battles that were never done
When honeybees would make us run

Maybe if we set aside
Human ego, selfish pride
Revisit where the woods can hide
Honeysuckles that grow inside

Inspiration

You'll find me in a Summer-scape
Fields are golden, you're beholden
To pursue me any place
Where sun and grace are olden
And also in the moonlit sky
Pardon me as I pass by
Whispering the lunar will
And resting on your windowsill

Taking Grace

Wasted years, days, and hours
Much of nothing to regret
Waste severe is to empower
Life that's something to forget

Plucking leaves and smelling flowers
Time well-spent and truly living
But much idle can devour
And prevent from duly giving

Are we spinning wheels in clay?
Attempting progress, yet prevented
Do we tell ourselves, today
To strive for less, forget incentive?

Can we all go on this way
Making haste to dine about?
Borrowing must come to pay
Taking grace when time runs out

Some Mornings

Some mornings I'm awake and clear
On others I can doze
Some mornings I've a song to hear
On others, just a prose
Sometimes I think I have it all
While oft I am in need
And other times I'm standing tall
Behind a paper creed

Some evenings I believe and trust
While other times I fear
Some evenings I've no carnal crust
But frequently in tears
As darkness comes I have a plan
Yet dreading its appeal
I make believe that I can stand
While falling to a kneel

Some nights my sleep is sweet as gold
While others I'm awake
Some nights I do as I am told
Yet tempted to partake
Awaiting morning fervently
My strength does not suffice
Apart from all uncertainly
With ever-present vice

For mornings, evenings, nights, and all
I hold this to be true
I'm predisposed to take the fall
Unless I trust in You
It's not that I'm unsoundly made
I'm just so incomplete
So while You work throughout the day
I'll rest in You and sleep

Everlasting Time

Lord, what precious, pleasant grace
'Tis sweeter smelling still
Than all the flowers in this place
Upon Thy holy hill

A reminiscent odor of
The miracle divine
Memories of lasting love
Forgiveness that was Thine

Though all creation sparkle bright
With vistas of allure
Yet none can shed the smallest light
Nor fragrance can secure

The feeling that we all retain
When minds are taken back
When Calvary and woe and pain
Put history on track

Our senses are accustomed to
Life's whims and all its ways
Not relative to things anew
Nor everlasting days

But when You hung for all to see
The world was standing still
And though among the few, I be
Yet sing Thy praise I will

A supernatural divide
A line drawn in the sand
To stay amongst the changing tide
Or follow with the lamb

I'll follow, Lord, until I shed
This body or this mind
I'll follow Thee as I am led
To everlasting time

Entropy Erosion

Admiring the dance of ivy
Stop and study for a bit
Knowing its direction might be
Unpredictable, but slightly
Looming through the chaos lightly
Seeing a design in it

Seemingly chaotic still
Is time throughout its motion
Eventually it will reveal
Direction of an agent's will
Verses from a careful quill
Entropy is in erosion

Like a vine is branching out
The passing days meander
Taking such a winding route
Loosely bound to turn about
On predictions casting doubt
And so revealing grandeur

Appalachia in the Fall

Brushed over with a reddish brown
And bits of yellow sprinkled in
Where leaves are scattered on the ground
Delivered by a chilly wind

When life is put on hold again
And business has been set aside
Nestled in a cozy glen
Or sat next to the fireside

A lovely little place to hide
And bathe yourself in skies of blue
Where you can take a mountain ride
Or paddle in an old canoe

Autumn can be good for you
And hills can elevate the season
Rocky streams and morning dew
Present a most compelling reason

Dangerous Serenity

While staring at the sky today I almost crashed my car
It's just, I couldn't look away
The pinks and oranges in array
A cotton candy cloud display
The setting sun has gone too far

Before another is entranced, we need to look away
The blending pastels so enhanced
I never even had a chance
Submitting me at my first glance
And filling me with words to say

And now I'm in captivity to beauty from afar
Not since my nativity
Was color seen so vividly
A dangerous serenity
Causing me to crash my car

Time to Pass

The bass are really jumping
Listen for the sound
Along with that of rustling leaves
Bubbling water and the bees
Squirrels that scurry in a hurry
Leaping through the trees

But now the moment's over
So I have to go
Work to do and bills to pay
Inconsequential things to say
Dreams to chase through outer-space
To waste away the day

Maybe if I'm ever done
Then I'll sit a while
Upon a little mossy grass
Pleasantly for time to pass
Waiting and anticipating
Jumping of the bass

Treasure

Mellow is the feeling when I'm walking
Yellow is the welcome day, orange upon return
Lavender, a taste of what I'm stalking
Traveler through fields of hay
Following the woodsy way
Treasure, my concern

Skylit are the trees throughout the evening
Violet is the ocean in the firmament above
Rapturing, the feeling I'm retrieving
Capturing the notion
Of heavens in their motion
The coloring of love

Witty Clue

Pictures never do it justice
Always something more to see
Neither can the words be trusted
To relay it faithfully

Painfully we try and fail
Striving to express in vain
Feelings that we might as well
Never bother to explain

So insane that we alone
Should carry such a memory
Pondering what we were shown
Gazing at the imagery

In simile and clever rhyme
We veil it in a witty clue
Lingering for such a time
Until the time that we are through

The Setting Sun

The evening sky was set ablaze
Suppose that I just stand here gazing
Clouds and colors, all amazing
It's perhaps the end of days

Preferred above the other ways
As fire is a certain cleanser
Coals from Heaven's golden censer
Vaporizing into haze

Being ready always pays
That something good would be left over
Apart from folly, something sober
Releasing into spectral rays

But now the sun a'yonder lays
Resting from a day of glowing
So I'll face tomorrow knowing
He whom all of time obeys

PART 2: *Regal Recollection*

Strange Addiction

Take a sip of loneliness
Accursed brew and bitter dose
Chase it down with apathy
Toward the ones you love the most

Drink until you're seeing ghosts
Slurring accusations past
Staggering away from moments
That were never meant to last

Spirits from a heavy glass
Linger in your consciousness
Terrifying are the feelings
That you know you can't resist

Sobering is all of this
Still you're coming back for more
Sorrow is a strange addiction
Letting go, the only cure

Brainstorm

Surely something airy levitates
Floating, barreling in streams
Of my consciousness innate
Or so it seems
When in dreams
Or in visions I partake
Of festivities so clever
That I never want to wake
From them ever

Life's Holiday

Dusty reels of memory
Like playing in the creek
And I can feel the summer breeze
It's laying on my cheek

The water cool, the weather warm
We rightly stayed outside
Until the coolness of a storm
And lightning made us hide

Back when we had trees to climb
And woodland trails to blaze
And with that the peace of mind
That children have always

I can almost feel it now
This summer on my skin
Oh that it were real somehow
To wander there again

Droplets

In a sweet remembrance, weak
Of all the things I shouldn't speak
Of all the bleak and hopeless pages
Waiting as I leak for ages

Losing liquid memories
In metaphors and similes
The remedy to isolation
Droplets of imagination

Lands Uncharted

On a quest for lands uncharted
Where the time has not departed
And the hours are preserved
Bottled up and undisturbed

There I heard a storyteller
Talk of moments in the cellar
Kept away from light and air
So that pilgrims can repair

Rugged wear of wasted years
Seasoning with different tears
Ones that fall as diamonds might
Sparkling in wisdom's light

Am I right to venture on?
Or are second chances gone?
Is it all too good to be?
I would pay in memory

Opportunities

Flowers do in patience wait
Dressing in their Sunday best
Pastels soft and so ornate
Searching for an eye to bless

Making so much more of less
Simple with a stately view
And for whom we do obsess
Paying homage that is due

A spectrum of the finer hue
Blending an organic ink
With little bits of red and blue
Yellow, purple, orange, and pink

Careful not to even blink
Moments have been known to pass
Opportunities distinct
Colors that can never last

Moments

Like cool waters on a hot day
And a shady place to sit and listen
A time to rest and ponder on
Our best and worst decisions

Reshaping what you could not say
In moments you have not been given
A chance to reevaluate your
Simple life and mission

Your life is not a vision
The march of time cannot be stayed
You don't get another shot
At choices that you've made

There's a contradiction
Between our feelings and our faith
You'd better think it over while
You sit down in the shade

Another Calvary of Today

I met a man that gave it all
Trying to redeem us, praying
In laying down his life I saw
The things that Jesus stood there saying

I saw a death put on display
I saw the nails and scarlet robe
I saw forgiveness in such a way
That can't exist throughout the globe

Revealing love and there presenting
Another mind that can't resent
A mortal man was representing
Naught but pure of heart intent

Was this Christ? Both yes and no
Another form, as you might say
And can we go so far to show
Another Calvary of today?

Danger

It seems as though the fire's burning
Hotter, hotter, lumber churning!
And expanding into space
That's outside of the fireplace

Embers chase and flames are licking
Hurry, hurry, time is ticking!
In my slumber I neglected
Danger that I once respected

I'll correct it, I'll repair it
Water, water, mustn't spare it!
Maybe I'll forego the dozing
Better not to know the hosing

Reminiscence

To savor life as tasting wine
Decadence for taste refined
Of setting suns and changing leaves
Of carelessness and joy simplistic
Also, of the intellect
In stimulation naturalistic

Deterministic though it seems
Yet mingling with mystic dreams
Of happenstance, time, and chance
Of optimistic calculation
Also, of the disconnect
Reality from expectation

Elevation and ascension
Memories too sweet to mention
Of love and loss, sentimental
Of tender mercy and conviction
Also, of the retrospect
Remembering the self-infliction

Morning Amore

Only just a cup of coffee
On an icy winter morning
And the sweet remembrance, too
Of everything you ever do
Behind my eyes, parading through
Softly in my mind adorning

Only just the scattered words
Arranged in such a way as this
Making them alive and true
A blended and a balanced brew
Causing me to think of you
Absurdly so, but I insist

Vagabond

Home sweet home, afraid I haven't
Doomed to roam an angry planet
Without room for those like me
I languish apathetically

How can it be that I could change
When opportunity is strange?
How can it be that I recover
Without father, without mother?

Is there another condescending
To the gutters I am trending?
I've come across a very few
Who understand what I must do

They bid me shoo and get away
To rid themselves of my dismay
And when I seek for bare provision
They entreat me into prison

But I've a vision, I've a dream
It's my mission to be clean
And though they think that I am lying
On the brink with nights spent crying

Those supplying all my need
Becoming such a dying breed
What used to be the helping hands
Now choosing just a passing glance

The chances of my life I ponder
Advancing me alone to wander
Lacking food and medication
Relapse to inebriation

Aren't we a nation speaking?
True sedation I'm still seeking
The creeping cold in patience waiting
The reaping hand of my sedating

Memories

Go easy on me, memories
And don't remind me of decisions
Carry yourself gracefully
Making most minute incisions

Surgically diluting visions
That long ago were tucked away
Hiding them with such precision
Keeping my regret at bay

Lying to myself today
Living in a mind frustrated
Trying to go on this way
Knowing that my smile is faded

Knowing that my view is jaded
And my will, completely spent
And it's like I first had stated
Memories live free of rent

Little Things

It always was the little things
Fragrant petals, feathered wings
Little strings you never pull
To keep from messing up the jeans

Remembering when coffee's hot
And soda's cold and hits the spot
When you have got a million years
To ponder on your life and lot

To tie the knot with happiness
And also pain, I must confess
It's such a mess, but little things
Alleviate a lot of stress

Carry Me

Pick me up and carry me
Carry me with tender touch
Tender touch and clever company
Is what I crave so much

Craving never satisfied
Satisfied by only glimpses
Glimpses into better times
Of safety within fences

Fences that could separate
Separate and so protect
So protect from anything
That children might inspect

Might inspect the hissing sound
Hissing sound that draws us in
Draws us in to bring us down
To selfishness and sin

PART 3: *The Clause of Charity*

Our Apostle

This life has got a hold on me
I swear if I could ever cut it loose
But it's tightening, I didn't get to choose
Like a noose, which is frightening
Because I fear my oxygen supply
Is the only thing that's keeping me alive
At a cost, at a penalty
At a fee of dangerous expense
Far too high for me to pay the recompense
So I'm meant for a pilgrimage
A lonely and a sorrow-stricken way
Where my heritage of thorns is on display
But another crown awaits, a reward
One for which I am inclined
To submit myself in body and in mind
So in time you will understand
That everything I'm doing is for you
And that everything I'm telling you is true
So I bid this world adieu
Yet it's needful I remain
For I know what I must do
And to die, for me, is gain

He's Been Showing

This life is but a test, I'm failing
Not so long ago, I passed
Where once I found myself prevailing
In time success just didn't last

It went too fast, what can I say?
Like sand in water, ever fleeting
Night has overtaken day
My plans and dreams are all receding

I sit here needing, never filled
Yet in a moment I'm reminded
Clearing thoughts, remaining still
Seeing through what once was blinded

I've refined it, no, not me
Another force outside my knowing
And being lifted, now I see
The hidden things that He's been showing

Another Fate

How clumsy that I must've been
To fall for sin completely
When in secret I had reveled in
The darker praise discreetly

So release me
Because I know that it doesn't do to dwell
But it's easy
When psychosis can be triggered by a smell

It's a mental show and tell
And a maddening descent
To a special kind of Hell
Where the devil would repent

Oh I hope you take the hint
So that you can never take the bait
To welcome my intent
Is believing in another fate

Where to Begin

Precious Lord, I come before you
But I don't know what to do
It seems as though they've looked to me
But I pointed them to you

They think that I have answers
And that I should lead the way
How unaware they all must be
I make it day-by-day

But Lord you're always here for me
To run to and to hide
I fear that in exalting self
I've led them all aside

I fear that in promoting flesh
I've led them to believe
Apart from seeking Christ alone
That they should look to me

That was not my intention
Yet intentions can be blurred
For when I fail to call on thee
And read thy Holy Word

That's when I fall and stumble
And so often it has been
That in my sad repentance
I don't know where to begin

But Lord I know that when I pray
You listen every time
And for some reason, yet unknown
You always ease my mind

I know I've caused you trouble
Far more times than I recall
But still you're always standing there
To catch me as I fall

How can men, so lifted up
Endeavor to declare
How they now understand the things
That only you can share

I'm seeing more and more that all
My knowledge is for naught
Because from you alone have I
Received that which I've sought

So Lord, one more time, help me
To remember what you said
And how it was for me
That precious, holy blood you've shed

And how I was in need
Because mankind is in a fall
As Paul said, "When it comes to sinners
I was chiefest of them all"

Higher to Shine

Amid daily life, with its wonder and glee
Emotions of limitless variety
Mingled together, like daylight and rain
Another clear spectrum of pleasure and pain

To suffer through sorrow, we all can expect
To face the dark nights of remorse and neglect
Confounded by seemingly meaningless woes
Which life has just only begun to expose

And just when you feel that it couldn't get worse
More specters of madness than Hell can disperse
Will visit upon you affliction and stress
With memories shamed, which you've tried to repress

And while in the midst of this battering storm
With masts all but broken and sails nearly torn
You peer up toward Heaven and ponder the cause
Awaiting an answer from God and His laws

Now at your wits-end there's a last-minute hope
A sweet revelation that helps you to cope
For why must the devil so focus on you
Unless to discourage from what you might do?

Oh what might you do, if left unassailed?
If Satan is scared that means you have prevailed
Oh what must he fear that he feels to distract?
He must have a kingdom that you can attack

Remember when pressure and strain have you bound
That surely in you there is strength to be found
The strongest of soldiers are on the front line
The brightest of stars are hung higher to shine

Playing Games with Hell

"This life is not worth living"
A distant voice will say
Yet growing ever closer
As you struggle through the day

"These things are not worth doing"
It says behind your back
Now so close you can't retreat
You have to interact

"Your goals are not worth reaching"
Your ear is now inclined
Subjected to this whispering
And giving of your time

"Your friends are not worth having"
No stranger anymore
The voice is sounding more like you
As reason you ignore

Why are we so vulnerable to
Strange voices in the night?
Why must we subject ourselves
To dark instead of light?

Why won't we just listen to
The still, small voice inside
Which reminds us to remind ourselves
Of purpose, love, and life?

It really is a mystery
We really do excel
In wading through the dreaded deep
And playing games with Hell

We know there's a solution
It stares us in the face
To stop and cast down all these thoughts
With scriptures to replace

Christianity

Truly amazing, undoubtedly true
A life that's worth living for me
Joyously praising and worshiping too
Finally praying for purpose anew
So mighty a tree, so many the fruits
With branches of strength
All born from a seed

Solely providing and presently here
A promise on which I believe
On chariots riding and pressing out fear
Oh so exciting and pleasantly near
So highly esteemed, such heavenly cheer
Delightfully sweet
A gift to receive

Relation Divine

There's doctors and lawyers and princes and such
Degrees of respect and renown
There's titles that praise and esteem us so much
From heights we can never come down

There's men's admiration and people's applause
A grand invitation to shine
There's wonderful splendor in basking in awe
Apparent relation divine

But of all the titles and reverent degrees
Just one I've desired so dear
And with opportunities here to be pleased
Through all I can see it so clear

To be called a brother, so wonderfully fair
The sweet recognition of grace
And to be considered as Jesus' heir
None other prestige can replace

The title of brother can carry a weight
Wonderfully, fearfully so
The responsibility ever so great
But blessed forever to know

That all of creation is groaning to see
A manifestation of truth
Far above nations and fortunes and kings
Preparing the places for you

Election

Far beneath the clutter and the melancholic sigh
Far below the apathetic wonderings of why
Further down and underneath a disappointed cry
Buried and submerged, a seed on which you can rely

Far away from hopefulness and longings to fulfill
Far apart from cleverly defining what is real
Further more aside from optimistic morning zeal
Lost and gone, the seed remains protected by a seal

Long forgotten thoughts that still inspire from afar
Longing to unearth the things that tell you who you are
Loneliness and burden may have left you with a scar
One thing is for certain, there's a seed inside your heart

All the layers of lethargy could never keep you down
All the distance in between can't keep from where you're bound
All of the uncertainly that's hardening the ground
Can't withstand a little seed, the gardening is sound

The Sons of God

They'll carve me in marble some day
I hope that my visage is put on display
In palaces fit for a king
Or else overlooking the mountains in Spring

And chance that I'm chiseled in bronze
For great contributions throughout the eons
I harbor a humble request
That down by the ocean they lay me at rest

Or maybe in paintings of oil
Where over the ages my colors will spoil
As others look on and admire
All of my glory in lofty attire

Perhaps I am reaching too high
But really, too low when you look to the sky
And notice the glittering jewels
Hovering over the kingdom He rules

Make Angels to Sing

Forgiveness is ringing, the angels are singing
What joyous occasion is this?

And now I hear clapping, I know I hear laughing
What reason is there for this bliss?

I'm seeking and searching, just frantically working
Oh help me, I don't understand

But then He speaks peace, I fall to my knees
I'm seeing the Master's great plan

The Shepherd has taken a hand
The Savior has offered His grace

The Heaven of heavens, anointed with glee
A saint has just finished their race

Another lost soul has come home
Another dear child of the King

A shackle has fallen, a captive set free
And this will make angels to sing

The Holy Grail

The Holy Grail, I've found it!
Or rather, it found me
Through all of time and history
An ever-growing mystery
As I stand here confounded
At the way things had to be

It's only a few pages
Some paper and some ink
And though it bears the stains of time
Preserved by only chance divine
But now by Heaven's graces
I have time to read and think

Foreknowledge

Bathed in a transcendent luminescence are the days
On which we are dependent, like the trees to solar rays

My eyes begin to glaze, my mind is captivated
As visions of the past amaze and leave inebriated

Memories inflated by a sense of déjà vu
Oh to be emancipated and to be with You

And to know it's true, and to be elected
Bringing into view a plan that nobody expected

Necessary Evil

Death is not selective in the pattern that it shows
Mostly open-minded as he watches in repose
Collectedly composed, not a show of nervous twitch
Patiently respectful, not discerning poor from rich

He'll leave you in a ditch or he'll strow you in the street
And also many other things that aren't quite so neat
He's really an elite, a creative and a wise
Coming from behind or even looking in the eyes

Appearing in surprise or the dreadful long-awaited
An unforgiving algorithm that he has created
Sometimes in a faded semi-merciful release
But seemingly indifferent to our merit in decease

Is there any peace for the antiquated soul?
An overarching justice from an angel on patrol?
Is it just a role that the reaper has to play?
A necessary evil, motivating all the way

Called to Help

Simon the Cyrenian was called to help one day
As a lonesome man of sorrows
Was walking on His way

Toward the dark Golgotha, there to lay His own life down
But that lonesome stranger stumbled
And His cross had hit the ground

I can't help but envy Simon, though I know not who he was
I can't help but wish that I were him
Because of what he'd done

I can't help but wish I had the chance to take upon myself
That blessed opportunity
To give the stranger help

Though none could see it clear that day, my eyes are open wide
Though none saw fit to sing His praise
My tongue shall lift Him high

Though all the world rejected Him, yet I'll not be ashamed
I'd cherish any moment
Just to suffer for His name

Oh Simon, angels smiled on you when you stepped up that day
And how I would give anything
To help Him on His way

His body was so broken and His strength was almost gone
But Jesus should have never had
To bear that cross alone

Perhaps someday I'll have the chance to share His heavy load
For lost souls, sick and dying
While along this lonesome road

For that man is no stranger, He's the precious Lamb of God
Whose mind was upon me
While on the lonely road He trod

PART 4: *Intellectual Evening*

Underneath

Underneath the greatest strain
Concussive pain and nerves are failing
Weeping, wailing, fall impending
Yet pretending, life's a game

Underneath a pressure daunting
And it's haunting how I'm feeling
And revealing deep intentions
What inventions I am flaunting

Underneath a love pathetic
You're aesthetic, I'm invested
So arrested by emotion
True devotion is poetic

Underneath an endless passion
Not in fashion, yet alluring
So enduring the sensation
My oblation and my ration

Intended to Adore

Until the approach of darkness
Comes to part us, we'll endure
Until death alone has scattered
Torn and tattered, we're secure
Until even space is rended
We've intended to adore
Until only time and silence
Reunite us evermore

Pressing Matters

I guess that all the stars aligned
I must confess, I hadn't noticed
Up until this very moment
I was bored with all the signs

But now the dots across the sky
Connect to form exotic creatures
Truly a historic feature
Prophesies are on the rise

A desperate world in horror cries
Begging for interpretation
Seeking only consolation
From a message in disguise

A shame I didn't recognize
Due to other pressing matters
First a splash and then a splatter
And my coffee's compromised

Capital

Writing never seems to pay the bills
Though in time it may
Diamonds are a mine away
Veins of gold are running underneath
Below the miry clay

A lottery of excavating hills
In the human sense
Digging for experience
Shoveling the acres of my mind
At my own expense

Fortune for the sake of my ideals
Would be fortunate
Maybe just a little bit
Capital for pressing ever on
Through the wilderness

What We See

We see what we want to see
And nothing more is meant to be
So we ignore the little things
That constitute reality
So let it be, and be as though
We needn't know what we don't know
And so it goes that we can just excuse
The gaps beneath our nose
A bit of prose
A pinch of literary daring, and we'll be
Along the way to showing unto others
What we didn't see

Writer's Block

I can't stand to write them anymore
I want to read them
And heightened are my senses to explore
That's why I need them

I'm longing to believe them
Flipping through the night and day
And hoping I'll retrieve them
Getting lost along the way

Strolling off, I want to stray
Following desire
Searching for the words to say
To throw them in the fire

On the Roll

A touch of university
And ego takes its toll
Your name is on the roll
With cognitive diversity
The selling of your soul
For reaching of your goal
Admission to fraternity
Submission to control

Carpe Diem

Life is not so temping as the appetite implies
A fact that stands to quell the hungry glimmer in our eyes
And though a youthful lust proceeds
Reality will yet impede
And serve us notice that indulgence drives until we die

Passing years accelerate, each swifter than the last
Until the future pales to be compared to all that's past
And though we may ignore the truth
That lust consumed our fleeting youth
Age will one day tell the tale of life that's gone too fast

And most unfortunate, that second chances don't exist
Time is such a current that the swimmer can't resist
We try to hold our head up high
While holding back a solemn cry
To think of opportunities we know that we have missed

These few somber words present a challenge to us all
Not to be depressive, but to help us to recall
That every day should be received
And every word of God believed
And even when we're falling there is beauty in the fall

Bitterness

Bitterness is such a root
To wicked trees with sour fruit
And pulling from this life, you find
The wilted rotting on the vine

You find a wine of bitter taste
From grapes where poison is encased
You find an inspiration grim
Just bubbling up to the brim

You find the stem a twisted sprout
It arrogantly spreads about
The flowers and their colors, fair
But putrid fragrance in the air

And though you care to till the ground
To see if vengeance can be found
You're better not to plant this seed
To harvest only selfish need

Because indeed at harvest time
When reaping this will make you pine
To see it overtook the field
And left no room for pleasant yield

There is a shield that can protect
And something better to expect
To sow forgiving seeds of love
Where sweet aromas rise above

Small Talk

Nervousness is not endearing
Anxiously awaiting, fearing
Comfort disappearing
With the clearing of my mind

Rearing up the motivation
Steering in a blind fixation
Tearing agitation
The sensation that I find

I never have the time
Forever I am running and evading
Neurology cascading
Pretending I am fine

Impending is the waiting
Charading and debating my disguise
With interest imitating
Creating my demise

Reaching Out

I'm reaching out
Through freezing rain or feet of snow
I'm reaching out
Defying what the wind can blow
I'm reaching out
Into the uncomfortable
I'm reaching out
I just thought you need to know
I'm reaching out
Although the frost has bitten me
I'm reaching out
Smitten with humanity
I'm reaching out
Treating you like family
I'm reaching out
Where's your Christianity?

The Winning Side

I'm filing for divorce from life
I've really had enough
So now I need another wife
That isn't quite so rough

I need an opportunity
To reset everything
To find a new community
Where no one knows my name

I'll need another place to live
And also one to work
I'll even need a name to give
As this one I will shirk

I'll have to have some hobbies, too
I mustn't sit around
I guess I'll find some things to do
While roaming through the town

And so I'll make some newer friends
With whom to share a smile
And then I'll find the latest trends
Adapting all the while

My secret plan is nearly done
I'm ready to depart
And though I pack my bags to run
I cannot pack my heart

It's true, escape can so appeal
But it would not resolve
And troubled times, though really real
Are destined to evolve

Alas, I know that I shall stay
And never run and hide
For though my thoughts may go astray
I'm on the winning side

Puddles on the Floor

Going through the motions doesn't cut it anymore
Motionlessly, aimlessly, impeding my believing
Believing in the prospect of my progress, and leaving
Leaving me in puddles on the floor

Society

Isn't it just natural
To feel the world is caving in?
A broken heart is casual
And par for course
From start to end
You mean that you didn't know
The creeping hand of apathy?
Well pardon me
I must be living
In my own society

The Fullness of Time

Brushed over with a reddish brown
And bits of yellow sprinkled in
Where blood is splattered on the ground
To separate a world from sin

When time is put on hold again
And judgment has been set aside
Nestled 'tween a thorny brim
And settled at the evening tide

A lovely little place to hide
And bathe yourself in words of truth
Where you can touch the other side
And there, partake of living fruits

This volume can be good for you
Seven seals to bring the season
Holy hills, eternal youth
Present a most compelling reason

PART 5: *Some Poetic Somethings*

Some Poetic Something

Writing isn't such a waste of time
Though I rot or either
Ripen on the vine
But to catch the fermentation
Right between the silver lines
How that some poetic something
Would articulate divine
By a loosely veiled connection
And a vivid fascination
Drawn from careful introspection
With direction of a rhyme
Something hopelessly magnetic
Is genetically inclined

Limited Time

Oh that I could sit in leisure
Humming to myself against the time
And not on pins and needles
From which I can't recline
How that levity would shine
And the brashness of the fraying
Of my nerves would all dissolve
In the fashion of my sayings
I would zealously evolve
But the half of me is graying
From the pressure
From the calling
At capacity I'm weighing

We Yearn

Aren't there more hours in the day?
Always pressing, always rushing
Always so much more to say
That the weight of it is crushing
And the state of it is gray
Like an overcasted sky
With an overdue display
Of the shining of the sun
To enlighten and inspire
Like the slowing of the clock
We so youthfully require
Never ready to retire
Never willing to return
Only steadily aspire
How incredibly we yearn

Wisdom & Wit

My timeless collection
Of beautiful things
An ocean of pages
To show for my wages
With closer inspection
Attention it brings
To wisdom and wit
Enticing to sit
With prophets and sages
Where candles are lit

Fairytales

Once upon a time
In a land that isn't really there
Fires rage and buildings crumble
Sigh - but we don't really care
Broken bones from wreckage stumble
Shelters for the lost and humble
Fall, but we are unaware
Very far away
With the children that do not exist
Bullets rip through bedroom walls
Citizens cannot resist
Nights are filled with siren calls
Futuristic cannon balls
Drop, but we can coexist

Just Like That

And just like that
I got what I had coming, and it came
Like a freight-train down the track
I was running, but in vain

I was stumbling away
Understanding the futility
But wanting to escape
From its inevitability

Knowing my fragility
And how it will bestow
Inescapable humility
Of reaping what you sow

In the fleeing you can't go
Anywhere it cannot find you
The penalty you owe
Just like that, it's right behind you

Emptiness

The blessedness of emptiness
Allegedly a cursing
I find myself traversing
Through time and space and memory
Repeatedly rehearsing
Departing from my comfort zone
Alone to quench the thirsting
For inspiration bursting
To know what I could not have known
I guess it's not the worst thing

Kind of Green

Of all the many things I haven't seen
They have me feeling kind of green
And for bringing me to tears
I'm awfully wet behind the ears
My experience is lacking
It appears
But determined
I am that, to say the least
Oh and keen to bridge the chasm
From the belly of the beast
To the burning of the Sun
In the dawning of the East
I have only yet begun
To appreciate the feast
Of the flavors of desire
And the spices of emotion
I admire
And the seasoning of bittersweet devotion
Cooked to promising perfection
Over unforgiving fire
Taken off before the burning
In the tasting is the learning

How Sublime

With certainty a burglary
To rid me of my sorrows, I endured
Such a robbery of all my insecurity, for sure
It has lifted and removed
All the partial unrefined
Incompleteness disapproved
Weighing heavy on my mind
I am liberated by a blessed crime
And the culprit is at large - how sublime
I'm not pressing any charges at this time

Pages in the Gutter

I could fill a book of many pages
And I will
I could settle by a brook, very still
And write for ages
Or with kettle or with pot
Brewing something, it's outrageous
The amount that I could jot
When the feeling is contagious
But to every silver lining is a cloud
And to every peaceful moment
Something boisterous and proud
To disintegrate the solace
Interrupting the occasion
Always something to befall us
And it's loud
With society's invasion
And I shudder to remember the ordeal
Just to utter of the books I didn't fill
And the pages in the gutter

Lonely Bones

Of myself alone I've lended
I come highly recommended
Suitable for such a favor
Be it knowledge, heart or labor

As a neighbor's open door
Come on in and so explore
And if you perceive I have it
Spare the niceties and grab it

Let your habit be to me
To access mine conveniently
I will at your service wait
To offer freely my estate

Solemn fate to meet your need
Spend me with a selfish greed
Then when you have bled me dry
Bid my lonely bones goodbye

Satisfaction

Just to satisfy the eye
I would guzzle in the waterfalls
And drink the rivers dry
I would breathe the upper atmosphere
And vacuum out the sky
Just to satiate the need
I would pluck the whole of vintage
Though you planted every seed
I would dash toward the heavens
With a luminescent speed
Just to offer my appeal
I would congregate reality
To share what isn't real
I would callus every finger tip
To challenge you to feel
Just to balance the ordeal

Another Chapter

Just another chapter to surpass
Some of laughter, some of shame
But alas, they are the same
Like the liquid in a glass
Half say empty, half fulfilled
I'm just glad it hasn't spilled
And contended with my grass
Just as green as it can be
Though the other side be greener
It's the heat without the shade
That isn't beating down on me
So I'll prefer the yellow blade
With the shelter of a tree

Former Days

Follow me along the way
Pressing onward, ever onward
Down a dusty path today
One that's grown and wanting wear
Where the traveler is rare
And the toll is seldom paid
I can hear from over yonder
As it were, the footsteps distant
From a time that's reminiscent
One in which we should have stayed
The alleviating pressure
Feeling lighter, ever lighter
As the country is arrayed
In the flowers of the summer
How they've stolen breath away
Follow me as I go back
Back in time to former days
And if I stumble for the captivating view
Or if by weariness I'm humbled
Maybe I can follow you

Restless

Just to contact you
With fingertips
How words could never do
As my nervous system radiates
In navigating through
All the impulses and signals
So that data can align
Into something that resembles
My forgotten peace of mind
Which is drowning in your suffocating eyes
As I'm concentrating
Trying to assemble my replies
But the flood of information
Like a surge
From which protection is denied
Always urging me to hide
I would turn in your direction
But it's turning me aside

PART 6: *Splash of Light*

Morning Palette

Green on top of blue
It's revealed to me by fire
Of the nuclear radiation
As I look up and admire
Which I do
Feeling perfect and entire
To release in meditation
All the things that I require
Just to clear a bit of space
And to free a bit of time to check the timing
As I race in my elation
To articulate the rhyming
And to season it with grace
And to show
That it needn't be embraced
Without appetizing flow
And to make another know
Of the mystery of light
How it travels in the morning
Just to magnify the sight
Of the waving of the leaves
Which are blowing off the dew
Where the coloring conceives
Of a green on top of blue

A Hundred Dragonflies

I swear there must have been
A hundred dragonflies, or more
In a moment it released me from my thinking
I was bounded to explore
While the wheels were slighting sinking
I was sure
That my swerving wouldn't cut it
Just to dodge the many more

That were flying from the woodwork
And the edges of the lake
As I'm crossing to the forest
And they're trying to escape
Never slowing
No precautions left to take
Just on-going, as though I had been
Allergic to the brake

In a miracle of chance, and a bit of
Quick maneuvering, I managed
Just to miss them with a dance
And to claim the clear advantage
So I hurried to the woods and up the creek
And like structure isn't present
In this poem
It was absent in my streak

Such a lesson that the scholars couldn't teach
That with just a hundred dragonflies, at least
And a sunny day with woods
And a lake, and a creek
You can make a bit of peace
With the pressure that disturbs
And exchange a ringing phone
For the singing of the birds

Nothing

Nothing beautiful
Nothing so refined
In the council of my solitude I find
I have nothing on my mind
Nothing colorful
Nothing even fair
In the treasured adoration of our care
There's a wilting in the air
It's an edict of divinity
Preventing the repair
For a season of affinity
To share
Such a message that enlightens our despair
That we sacrifice the nothing
Which deceivingly arrested us
Exchanging it for something
That in love has only tested us

Digging Deep

Like water is a force that never slows
This is carving out my mind
So my history's exposed
And the layers of sedimentary
Accumulated sand
From the hour glass that's draining
Into canyons that are grand
I don't mean to be complaining
Only so you understand
How that memory is dated
By the fossils of belief
And ideas are excavated
Like a treasure underneath
I can hardly stand the absence of relief
though a skull would be my pleasure
I would settle for some teeth
Just to justify my efforts
In a desert full of grief

Called & Chosen

The light is just too bright
I can't approach unto it
Though I feel a relativity
It blinds me if I do it
To jeopardize my sight
And travel without senses
As I seek familiar mystery
Abandoning defenses
Just the faintest touch
And how the mighty fountains of the deep
Are broken open
And torrential rains can weep
How a storm can softly speak
What I never could have spoken
All that's left for me to offer is my heart
Which thou hast broken
I can sense that it is time for me to start
There was never a decision
You just tore it all apart
With your collision

The Hidden Eden

For sitting by a brook
It's often colder than it looks
Though bluest skies are such for lighting
Greenest grass is so inviting
I'd almost swear the fish are biting
But through the window I mistook
What appeared to be
Such a captivating pleasantry
A broken promise of the eyes
Who's lies were in the seventies
But now a dip in expectation
Makes me turn around to find a coat
It's like when weeds are never planted
They just grow
It's like when flowers and their seeds require
Such a tender watering with care
Along with softest soil
And a bit of luck to ever share
A bit of color and success
But the weeds without the watering
Are fruitfully as blessed
So in nature, so in life's eternal test
That we find the hidden Eden
While ignoring all the rest

Praying for Death

Breath is often wasted on a prayer
Not that praying is a waste
But forgive me if I scoff at the affair
When the heart that should be rended
Is the one that doesn't care
And the character I'm playing
Isn't playing with me fair
And it's not what I intended
Oh how carelessly I'm saying
All the words that have suspended me
On altars where I'm laying
The improper way I'm praying
It's a mess
One of tears and disappointing
Bitter failures, I confess
But a touch of the anointing
Can alleviate the stress
How I know that You are dying just to bless
But I'm busy with the living
Where I'm dying, more or less

Running

Paralyzing thoughts
The kind that curl your toes
And make you hide under the covers
How I really run from those
The ones that can expose
A life of insecurity
I'm dodging them assuredly
Assuring that they never get the chance
To captivate my vulnerable mind
Holding me in trances that I struggle to unbind
Forcing me to settle and rewind
Erasing out the light
I'm racing from the demons of the night
I'm seeming like a failure
And then seemingly I'm right
Or maybe it's a voice that I should heed
An overwhelming choice
The battle I am destined to concede

The Peace

The peace is in forgetfulness
An absent-minded dream
Like the Sun is in a beam
And the colors of the flowers
Are the best that I have seen
How they decorate the hours
And extrapolate the rest
When my mind is in a nest
And the tangling inside of me
Has put me to the test
Though I designate reality to tears
I can smile in my delusion
While I'm bleeding from the ears
So I'm drawing the conclusion that my fears
Are illusions
And reality is bound to disappear
The intrusion of the malady
Has proven too severe

Oceanside

Maybe I'm oceanside
This is all a dream
I can hear the crashing waves
How they're saving me
From driving me insane
And perhaps that isn't traffic
It's the squawking of the gulls
Just identifying fish
I'll grab my poles
Any chatter that resembles a demand
Must be taken as the children
That are playing in the sand
I in desperation manifest the grand
Stick my fingers in my ears
And interpret it as such
But the visions of my head
Seem to trouble me so much

Beguiled

Lest we dare to interrupt the precious silence
Or allow internal struggle
Though it's subtle, to beguile us
For if ever there were time to recollect
For a moment, measured tender
It would render us respect
And with carefulness we try to understand
Why that every fleeting hour
Can't empower our demand
Such a vanity has captured once again
By disturbing our ascension
With the mentioning of sin

Unfinished

It's like I'm writing, but I'm not
Every effort is exciting
But it doesn't hit the spot
Every beautiful beginning, 'til the end
Is immutable
But thinning in its calculated trend
So I'm having to rescind
By considering the blend of my appeal
In a hopefulness to steal
From the something never penned
And the treasure I conceal
But I'm steeping it in pleasure
'Til it's ready to reveal

Double-Minded

Waning to a wilt
But I'm waxing to a bloom
With certainty I'm certainly
Allergic to the room
Encouraged to resume
And with a sense of urgency
The wiping of the guilt
Like it was an emergency
Thoughts are an insurgency
I could never bother to explain
And neither do I suffer to be bothered
It's a shame
For I am both defense and the aggressor
The greater and the lesser
The victim and the only one to blame

Late Spring

It's beyond my common hearing
Masterful in engineering
And endearing as a prose
Moving me like no one knows

How it throws me into trances
Pulling me for second glances
Of expanses that delight
Captivating day and night

I invite the quiet few
Those who listen as I do
To pursue the wilder things
From the view of tire swings

How it brings an opportune
Moment which expires soon
Yet the tune can still be heard
Whispering with every word

Savoring the Days

I open up my eyes
And it's like the Sun is rising in the skies
Like a long-forgotten knowledge
Is enlightening the mind
Like a moment of forgiveness
Is rewriting the unkind
Like I just forgot to find
And reason or excuse
For the demons of misuse
To direct me or deter me
Through a season of abuse
Ok maybe it's dramatic to deduce
That another day arriving
Is like angels on the loose
Or civility surviving
But I'd rather be excessive in my praise
Than ungratefully regressive
By not savoring the days

To Be Continued….

About Wheelsong Books

Wheelsong Books is an independent poetry publishing company based in the ocean city of Plymouth, on the beautiful Southwest coast of England. Established by poet Steve Wheeler in 2019, the company aims to promote previously unheard voices and encourage new talent in poetry. Wheelsong is also the home of the Absolutely Poetry anthology series, featuring previously unpublished and emerging poets from around the globe.

Publication List

- Ellipsis (2020) by Steve Wheeler
- Inspirations (2020) by Kenneth Wheeler
- Sacred (2020) by Steve Wheeler
- Living by Faith (2020) by Kenneth Wheeler
- Urban Voices (2020) by Steve Wheeler
- Small Lights Burning (2021) by Steve Wheeler
- My Little Eye (2021) by Steve Wheeler
- Ascent (2021) by Steve Wheeler
- Dance of the Metaphors (2021) by Rafik Romdhani
- Into the Grey (2021) by Brandon Adam Haven
- RITE (2021) by Steve Wheeler
- Absolutely Poetry Anthology 1 (2021) by Absolutely Poetry Group
- Absolutely Poetry Anthology 2 (2022) by Absolutely Poetry Group
- War Child (2022) by Steve Wheeler
- Hoyden's Trove (2022) by Jane Newberry
- Shocks and Stares (2022) by Steve Wheeler
- Autumn Shedding (2022) by Christian Ryan Pike

We have other poetry publications in the pipeline! You can read more about Wheelsong Books and its growing stable of exciting new and emerging poets on our website:

www.wheelsong.co.uk